Gosse Bluff and His Circle

John Watson

Gosse Bluff
and His Circle

Gosse Bluff and His Circle
ISBN 978 1 76041 689 8
Copyright © text John Watson 2019

First published 2019 by
GINNINDERRA PRESS
PO Box 3461 Port Adelaide 5015 Australia
www.ginninderrapress.com.au

Contents

Preface	7
Foreword	9
Gosse Bluff	11
Interlude at Lake Vanishing	56
Tabula Arata	62
Recollections of Hugh Edwards	78
Appendix: Further Fragments	83

Preface

Last night I dreamt I went again to the Upper Room
(Or, rather, all that's left of it today
So great the impulse to demolish and rebuild).
Here once had been a floor of pictured tile,
Mosaic showing panels from our history:
Here Actaeon is seen turned to a stag
Which then is chased by native dogs through banyan trees;
Here Daphne turns into a stringy-bark;
Here Zeus is represented as a shower of gold
And Danae falls back under wattle flower;
And here white sailors stealing aboriginal fire
Break from their border into treeless plains:
The central panel may have shown the Nullarbor
Across which climbs the sun as thylacine
Only at dusk to vanish. These, and many more
I could not quite recall or understand,
I'm sure were here in those now vanished ballroom days.
Fragments of frieze survive. One border shows
Men fishing in the stream which now flows underground
Towards the Quay. Another seems to show
A shimmering lake bed, dry and grassed, with grazing sheep
And Cyclops lazing in the winter sun.

Now through a window framed with scaffolding
(Rebuilding operations temporarily have ceased
And rust stains spread across the sandstone sill)
I see a glimpse of harbour, luminous with rain.
I danced here with a girl who once had danced
With a man who danced with Philippa Dubois. And here
James Benson and his sister first met Gosse;

Quite possibly Hugh Edwards wrote here on the wall
Against which Clara Wood leaned, sipping tea.

Biography is detail, nothing more;
Two things – *the tenor of the times and character*
May seem to give these details unity.
Yet if the times are recent and fragmented, then
The first may still be too diffuse to serve;
The second has, since Bradley, been discredited.
So, offered here are scattered incidents,
Some fragments from a paving largely worn away.

Foreword

The Galleria was a coffee house
In Rowe Street, Sydney, now long since erased.
My passion for what might be called
The Galleria Group began
Near Wentworth Park. My father once
Had taken me to tennis courts
Or idle water, near White Bay,
And on the way had pointed out
A large brick wall with chalked designs.
It was Hugh Edwards' 'maze of words'
Which even as we passed again
That very afternoon had changed.
I later learned more of this man;
My father thought him one of those
Who spoke in the Domain: Marxists,
Flat Earthers or the monitors
Of Visitors from Outer Space.
I didn't understand that wall
But tried to memorise the words
And hoped one day to find out more
Of H.R. Edwards. This in turn,
Although the links were tenuous,
Led me to Gosse, and Theo Zeus,
James Benson and his sister Jane
And Philippa Dubois. And then
By several serendipities
I met the son of Gosse J. Bluff
Who graciously, unstintingly,
Plied me with letters, manuscripts
And photographs, and with his wife

Encouraged me in my research.
For this I offer grateful thanks,
No less for memorable repasts
Of vichysoisse and pear flambé.
I thank also librarians
In Sydney's many libraries
Too numerous to itemise,
Particularly Valerie Bloom
For blissful hours as she unlocked
The secrets of the Archive Room.

Gosse Bluff

I

An early memory

A kangaroo in topiary, mown grass,
A shadow spreading at its hopping pace
Across the field beside the swimming pool.
The splash above the pool hangs in the sky
Defying gravity which Gosse as yet
Knows nothing of. The splash is like the crest
Of preening cockatoos. The sunset ends.

His mother indefatigable

His mother travelled often, in one day,
From Strathfield in the west to Circular Quay
And thence by packet steamer through the Heads
And up the coast to Broken Bay. By dray
Towards dusk she reached the scented hinterland.
At once she dressed, drank tea and left again,
That same night dancing at the Gosford Ball.

Walking

From her, Gosse took the mantle, *traveller*,
Although contracted to the human scale
Of walking, say, from Bronte to Bondi,
Enjoying heliocentricity
And stopping at the coliformous baths
To gossip there while cooling beer in ice
Which then was thrown into the pitching pool.

A later fondness for swimming

And here he'd swim with ice peaks in the pool
And lean at ease against the whitewashed walls
In fumigating sunlight. Here he met
John Kendall, nephew of the illustrious
Dactylic Kendall, who as they relaxed
Told him of sugar-cane, and heat, and birds,
And secrets of the Shark Arm Mystery.

Milkman

Some ancient accident of parish plans
Had meant the house now jutted on the road.
The milkman used to lean across the sill
Beside his horse, and ladle from a pail
A stream of milk outpouring like a sail.
One day his horse reached through the window too
And nudged the jug from this white rainbow's end.

Headlights

His taste for mystery may originate
In memories of the headlights of a car
Which turning at the distant paddock gate
Sent widening beams to climb his bedroom wall,
Then hover at the ceiling, fan, and turn,
Divide, and shimmy down the opposite wall
To linger in the dressing-table glass.

Often-repeated waves

'Make something more of that,' his mother said
(Ironically of course) whenever he
Might break away towards the banksia fringe
And see the distant lonely coastal wave.
And even now he feels discomforted
If ever he emerges from the dunes
To see again that same repeated wave.

A ginger beer plant

The bed is huge with quilted eiderdown.
His mother wears a faded floral coat;
She carries water in a wooden pail.
His catalogue of memories unfolds:
Along a gravel road in century heat
He had to bring a stoppered bottle home,
A ginger beer plant fizzing in its sand.

Swallows

The river floods, the café owner nets
A bucketful of yabbies in the street.
A teller from the bank in long, white sleeves
Stands on the steps and smokes a cigarette.
Outside the tennis courts beyond the town,
His bicycle against a thorn bush near the road,
He sees the water threatening swallows' nests.

The search for identity

'I wanted to make sense of all the past,
And from an early age I'd ask them all
To tell again those shards of narrative –
How one had carried water from the dam
Or went barefoot to school through drifts of snow,
And how another always knew the day
When swallows marshalled, leaving for the north.'

Conception at Gosse Bluff

'My mother was elusive but not coy.
I used to ask her where I was conceived;
She'd laugh, "You came down in a shower of rain."
At last one day she named the place, perhaps
Embarrassed that my name derived from it.
She'd travelled with my father there in drought,
Only to be surprised by sudden floods.'

His name explained

'She told me freely of that circumstance:
Gosse Bluff was like a wine-red oatmeal bowl
Ten kilometres wide. In red-shift time
A comet had dredged it in a single blow.
And now they'd watched the sunset bruise with cloud;
I was conceived and tentatively named
When first sweet-smelling rain pock-marked the dust.'

Night swimming

'We used to swim at night from Circular Quay
And sometimes had to dive hard to avoid
The suction of a turning ferry's spume;
And when we heard talk later of *Five Bells*
We thought we may have been there on that night
When Joe Lynch with his pockets weighted down
Dived heavily from one world to the next.'

Alfred Street

The Quay in those days still had rocks and planks
And fishermen and tidal dark at night
And splashing light like phosphorous dragonflies,
And small boats anchored, drifting just offshore.
And in the milk bars facing Alfred Street
Whose neon lights spilled out into the dark,
The jukebox could be programmed from each booth.

Mermaids

The phrase 'in those days' always haunted him;
The present thinly veiled a Golden Age,
And Past Imperfect was the floating barge
On which significance strutted the stage.
One night when workmen talked beneath a flare
He saw dark mermaids swimming close inshore;
A calm had settled like a tidal lull.

1945

Throughout the fireworks and the tears which saw
The end to all hostilities, Gosse was
Embraced and kissed a hundred times
(Once by a gentleman in tails), and danced
With several different partners, smelt perfume,
And gained forgetfulness waltzing with one
Who smiled her name Terpsichore as they danced.

The Earthquake Centre

The river, choked with water hyacinth,
Bamboo and aniseed, convolvulus,
Still managed to emerge and linger near
The Earthquake Early Warning buildings. Here,
A mile from where Gosse lived, through reclaimed land,
One day he found amongst oxalis flowers
Old seismograph sheets yellowed in the sun.

Ideas of coincidence

In settings such as this he first surmised
The place of randomness, coincidence;
Near these laboratories he walked where grass
Stood high with lace-cap heads in flowering discs
Like cells dividing in a microscope.
And here, quite unexpectedly he came
On what was once a painter's studio.

Impact damage

A smell of hops, storm clouds, pale bindweed flowers,
A castor-oil plant, birds' nests of bamboo
Hung heavily on this abandoned place.
Inside, Gosse saw a pile of magazines,
Rain swollen; table, chairs, a vase of straw,
And in the glow of fibreglass there stood
A world globe dented from an ancient fall.

A weir

Outside, he walked through flowering cassias;
Where bee hives stood near drums of kerosene,
A path mowed recently led to a weir.
Behind barbed wire the seismic bunkers stood,
Their sensors swathed in spiral milk-glass cones.
The darkening willow leaves like hanging hair
Moved as the first fine rain printed the stream.

Events proffer themselves

The task he chose, or eagerly embraced,
Was to explain a certain category
Of loose phenomenon, the 'accident',
The random, code unreadable, event:
Beside a boat house someone smokes, a child,
One arm in bandages, looks up just as
Sea birds attack a kite quite suddenly.

His response

And all of this should not entail resort
To long-defunct surrealism. So
He sought to lay out on a table all
That happened and precisely as it did
(A willow wand just brushing on the stream
Without disturbing insects walking there),
A still life of events he could depict.

Background blurring

His first recalled affection: pale smocked May
Was standing on a swing and standing still.
The rest – the stream, the landslide, quarry wall
Rock-face surmounted by a row of pines,
The quite particularly scattered cloud,
Then sunset like a memory of the sun,
The rest – and this was all the world – was blurred.

The expulsion

The sun shone brightly on the cabbage palms
And distant jig-saw of the sea through trees.
With youthful May, Gosse overstayed the time
Or failed to satisfy some minor rule:
The expulsion was polite yet firm, and quite
Irrevocable. They had to leave at once
And always felt they'd left themselves behind.

An emu enforces their expulsion

'We're looking back, and see behind bamboo
The cabbage palms above the railing fence.
We're studying the by-laws on the gates.
An emu stops and peers out through the bars;
The feather grass enjoys its own light breeze…
Then some official steps out on the lawn
And emptying a teapot cries, "Have fun."'

Gosse and May meet years later

And after the expulsion there began
The struggle to retrieve that Absolute
Which in that former garden they had known
Before they plunged into the Relative
And went their separate ways until, too late,
They met again in gardens dark with rain
And shared a rainy day in London town.

Elements of myth intervene in nostalgia

Rain had been falling heavily. In dark
Familiar London mist each visited
The same Botanic Gardens, each to see
Wattle in flower, the flowering eucalypts.
By accident's unknowable design,
In Kensington in sunlit rain both saw
Draped on the tree a drenched but golden fleece.

II

The Galleria era

In Rowe Street in the upstairs Galleria
Throughout the fifties many pleasant hours
Were spent debating if and in what sense
The acorn may be said to be an oak.
Much favoured too that *chestnut* (Gosse approved):
The puzzling, dazzling status of the world
And all that could be thought to be out there.

A Rowe Street regular recalled

'Coincidence! we always used to say,
Alluding not to those contrived events
In fiction oiling its exigencies,
But to the simultaneous happening
Of all that happens at a given time,
"The flotsam one wave spreads across our shores."
This figure we called *Benson's Paradox*.'

James Benson

With sister, Jane, born 1932.
Grew up on islands off the eastern coast;
His parents lighthouse keepers; sheep as pets;
A labyrinth of paths through auburn grass;
Habitué of Rowe Street and the Exchange
(Now sadly gone); Joint Holder of the Cant
Award for Longest Specious Argument.

The mystery of Identity

'Politics,' cried Benson ordering tea,
'Is scuba diving in a reedy lake:
The turbid flow of public life,
The imposition of restrictive categories…
I would prefer to view this manic century
As a many-coloured coat with which to dress
The mystery of intact identity.'

Pleasures

With Benson Gosse went diving off the coast;
By night they talked of puzzling paradigms
But day brought greater pleasures undersea:
The absence of all dialogue, the dense,
Oppressive wordless water mass on glass
And bubbles, silent, meaningless, benign,
The absence of all propositional forms.

The silence of the sea

Throughout their friendship when the times devised
A world bizarre, irrational, extreme
It was for them made intermittent by
The silence of the sea. Diving with tanks
Of oxygen they'd lose all sense of sound,
Then surface to the sirens from a barge
And soon the clamour of the century.

First marriage of James Benson

An early love Gosse saw in company –
Until his friend one weekend married her.
And yet within a month Gosse had become
Friend to them both, then loved as suddenly
James Benson's sister, Jane. In her he saw,
In her resemblance to his first love's love,
The lineaments of satisfied desire.

Gosse speculative

Gosse smiled. 'And what in woman we desire
Is vague uncertainty, that of the faun –
As if the mariner's naked figure-head
Were turning always from a single course
And contradicting our false purposes,
And even stepped down to the deck and walked
Amongst us, looking further out to sea.'

A French cultural ambassador

In London Gosse had seen the cool, serene
And beautiful *Europa* of Poussin
And felt himself deflected from himself
To be an advocate of French *mesure* –
Whose chief exponent at that time he thought
Puig-Aubert who, puffing on a fag,
Would saunter up and kick the winning goal.

Benson identifies cultural cringe

'We were still breaking from our emu egg;
Its dark, tough shell was difficult to pierce.
It was I think precisely at this time
That Menzies did but see her passing by
And innocence lay like a glaucous scale
Across the harbour here, and spread inland,
And blinded us to landscape as it was.'

Illuminations

A dusk illumination in a field:
Although the sun had set behind its crest
The light increased and lingered still. Perhaps
This radiance was shining from a cloud?
And should Gosse add this to his growing list
Of Uncaused Happenings? Could the beautiful
Be simply what is apparently uncaused?

Benson returns

A curious incident at the Galleria:
A girl like a gazelle – by this I mean
Tall, lean and pale – sat with a friend. She wore
What then was called a 'sundress' leaving bare
Her freckled back like speckled eland flanks.
Benson approached without embarrassment:
'I'd like to touch your back… Let me explain.'

The proposal elaborated

'I ask this in the name of science, or
To be more accurate, philosophy.
I postulate a link between the *touch*,
The mutual transfer through the epiderm,
And certain puzzling transitivities,
Those boundaries which give rise to paradox
Where categories appear to overlap –'

The experiment negotiated

'These may of course be visual, as in
The sense of drowning in another's gaze
(You might agree to this another time),
But first I seek your help in this experiment
(And, for her kind indulgence, thank your friend)
Simply to let me place my outstretched hands
Upon the moonlit sands of this calm shore.'

Second marriage of James Benson

In fact, this strange encounter led at last
To Benson's marriage, *to the subject's friend*:
One day he woke and startled by the knock
Unlocked the door with some surprise to find
Her standing smiling, with a holly branch,
The cautious friend, the unexamined back
Which would in time reveal its olive skin.

On the name Clara

That friend was Clara Wood (whose parents had,
In expectation of a boy, and curious
That no boys ever seemed to have been named
Clarus, were now resolved upon the name,
But honouring that Clara who played Brahms
Were quite content to feminise the form).
This Clara played, instead, plurality.

Clara Wood and paradox

In Clara, 'generous multiplicity'
Was happily allied to Benson's love
And love of paradox. Thus she endorsed
Those paradoxes of identity,
And those of body/mind duality,
Which, with the light's stop-frame complicity
She too embodied in her nakedness.

Childhood of Clara Wood

Pictures and china regularly fell
From wall and shelf, time-tabled on the hour.
The dogs would hear each train a mile away
But not the bantams who would scatter when
The Riverina Daylight thundered through.
This cottage, inches from the glittering line,
Saw Clara Wood's arrival in this world.

James Benson, sceptic

James Benson questioned childhood memories.
With Clara he returned to his own past.
That hill he had remembered as immense,
Jagged, with half eroded conifers,
And excavations like an overhanging cave,
Was now a slight incline, with straggling trees,
Which just escaped the flooding of the plain.

James Benson, critic

Whenever asked, 'Do you align yourself
With one or other of the major Schools
Of Thought on Narrative in Painting, Art
For Art's Sake, Realism?' he would say,
'Well, actually, I don't know much about art,
But certainly I do know what I'd like:
I'd like to meet the models for these works.'

Jane Benson, her story

While polymorphous Clara entertained
A startled James, now patient as the air,
Surprised by his own sudden gravity –
His sister moved through fads and fancies, soon
To leave them all behind by meeting Gosse,
Descending from the tunnel into light
Like mountain trains emerging at the coast.

Modernism in Australia

Jane Benson (as recalled by Millie Vane,
A fellow student at the Institute
Whose painting on a monumental scale
Susannah Laughing with the Elders was
Regarded as most scandalous) had once
When painting from the model shocked the school
By rendering the figure as still life.

Further confirmation

Vanilla Reith-Jones knew her at that time:
'I was a student then and modelled for
A group who did life drawing on the beach
Below the zoo. (It was secluded there.)
Jane Benson was a member of that group.
One day she startled everyone (and me)
By setting up a table and some fruit.'

Turbulent times

Her brother introduced her to a group
Who, from a distance, following Gurdjieff
Extolled the powers of breathing cow manure
And sleeping over straw. Asceticism
Alas, imposed itself too ardently,
For painting suffered and they could not find
Effective paths out of the abstract woods.

Passionate doubts

She painted with a definite charm, but shared
The passionate doubts which marred that circle; this
And, anxious to bestow upon mankind
The Spiritual, which she bore to excess,
She laboured to depict the sweat of work
And celebrated workmen digging holes,
Erecting scaffolding or raising roofs.

Social conscience

She disapproved of Streeton's quarry scenes
Precisely since he obviously preferred
The topographic to the human. She
Would have applied, as paint, her *reverence*
(See in particular *Miners* or *The Crane*)
And broached the *barricades mystérieuses*
By painting noble workmen storming them.

Turning point

But when Jane Benson met her brother's friend
She was perhaps already wearying
Of noble labour and the glistening arm,
And warmed to his uncertainty and vague
Determination not to dogmatise;
From seeing others as embodiment
She found in him the charm of vacancies.

III

Onset of affection

They walked along a winding granite gorge;
She turned and kissed his eyes impulsively
And drew the snaking river like a raft
Behind her, hawser twisted with her hair
Across her shoulder. Next, the waterfall
Soon followed and the landslide far upstream;
And everything that was not her lost ground.

The waterfall

She always was determined, passionate;
And when with Gosse in winter's saxe-blue light
She came upon the frozen waterfall,
The final flow's arrest in cracks and groans,
She wanted more than this. She wanted Gosse
To walk across the thin projecting glass,
And wanted too to burst this with a cry.

Some months later Gosse returns

'The day seemed closed, sealed like an envelope
Until I left the train, and then it flared
And flowered with addenda, afterthoughts,
Ideas of such dissolving, melting power,
I stood a long time knocking at the door:
A simple table shone beneath a lamp
Set out with bread, a vase of cornflower blue.'

Resolution

'She asked me in reluctantly, yet smiled.
The moment seemed momentous, made of stone
As if we watched Ayers Rock form on the plain.
I still remember now the table: flowers
Of bower-bird blue, some bread, a cup and bowl.
I almost cried, "*Don't alter anything!*"
I stayed that night and never thought to leave.'

Jane's recollection

'At first I didn't know he had returned.
I wasn't well; I almost didn't rise
At his insistent knock. I would have slept.
I'd laid the table with a linen cloth,
Some bowls, a loaf, cornflowers in a vase.
I was annoyed. I rose. Outside was dusk,
Pale conifers, the faintest cirrus sky.'

Gosse ponders contemporary events

What else was happening as those cornflower stems
Like lovers stood beneath their forest blue?
A fisherman perhaps reeled from the Heads
Some fragments from a Time Capsule, washed out
To sea: some public sentiments in verse;
A picture of Jean Shrimpton at the Cup;
A ticket from the final Bondi tram.

Again

What else? What else gained its significance
By happening as this vase stood on its cloth,
Its cornflowers like blue sea anemones?
That last tram went through moonlight to Bondi
Where, midnight blue, the sea appeared when waves,
Waving, knelt down in turning headlight flares,
Then disappeared again as cars drove on.

And again

And elsewhere in the world, what else – as blue
Cornflowers yielded up the palm to her?
The boats which called along the Hawkesbury's banks,
Heavy with peaches, milk, tomatoes, eggs,
Brought down past Lion Island to the Heads
And to the Markets – they were plying then;
And now perhaps one edged along the coast.

A grove

'We walked between the strawberry trees. We smiled.
The shadow of one palm just reached the base
Of one some distance further on and made
The puzzle of a shadow upside down...
We seemed to enter Nadar's *View of Pines*:
A sward with pines like emus clustering
In gelatin and bromide fixed on glass.'

The house revisited years later

'A white magnolia, with its lemon air
And large-coned flowers, used to shade the porch.
There used to be a swing, a summer-house,
Stacked firewood. The bower-birds have gone.
A motorway divides the further field.
But still the river winds obligingly
Allowing house and barge both to remain.'

Questionable elements in Gosse's character

It is a fact perhaps not widely known
That Charlie Chaplin, in a Little Tramp
Impersonation Contest once came third;
And Blaise Cendrars (whose made-up name Gosse liked)
Pretended to have danced with Chaplin once
Beneath the trees in spring in Montparnasse.
Gosse too inclined to such transparencies.

Further doubtful claims

Gosse liked to speak of days now legendary,
When he had flown in Howard Hughes' *Spruce Goose*:
'It was,' he'd say, 'a kind of ballroom floor
Sprung on the upthrust of the streaming waves.'
And sometimes he implied that for a time
He'd lived like the Chevalier d'Eon.
These must be listed under doubtful claims.

Gosse justifies his evasiveness

'What was it that perplexed me, stayed my hand
From fixing things in any final form?
It was that something quite articulate,
Intrinsically unique, should nonetheless
Gain its identity by fanning out
Into the indifferent world of difference
And lose itself in multiplicity.'

From a diary

'Affections sometimes fly from us and form
An almost palpable cloud above our heads
Like those reported out-of-body states
In which a person – like a speech balloon –
Against the ceiling sees himself below.
Such things have made me think *Nature adores
A vacuum*, feeling my own flight from self.'

Gosse and Jane travel

The distance beckoned; everything became
A vindication of Vitruvius,
Perspective's vanishing point: the light appeared
To quiver with the furthest headland's mass.
The air invisible yet filled with spray
Reminded him of childhood's first cartoon:
'A picture of a plane just out of sight.'

Along the Bight

Beside the coast he saw in Jane, by chance,
The intimations of Narcissus: cliffs
Spread endlessly to east and west, the spray
Became a listless point in distant haze.
The ochre cliffs stretched on without a beach.
He saw her look with fierce defiant gaze
Demanding light's reflection back to her.

Solitude encourages pretension

'All solitude encourages illusion.
Deserted coastal waves pounding the shore,
Desultory, lingering before they fell,
Embodied – gathered – in this lonely place,
The presence of the outer world, hard-pressed
Against the membrane that would separate
It from the observing, fluctuating self.'

A delicious illusion

And once in passing from the tree-less cliff
And down an ancient path he thought he saw
A scene resuscitated from the past,
A tableau of illusion: on the beach
Were Conder ladies holding parasols
Which, as he stepped on to the beach, became
Mere condors, mutton-birds, white pelicans.

Travel notes: leaving the coast

'The sky seemed absent, cloudless, inchoate,
Non-verbal. Interest centred on the ground,
Moss-agate flocculate or curd, the stain
Of chromolithographic paper. Here
Lay objects like a scattering of coins.
It was an ancient earth, unscoured by glacier
Yet cracked and peeled where frost transcribed its text.'

Travel notes: the air

'A sound like aeroplanes unseen, soon gone,
Intruded like a hypodermic point.
The air unblinking nowhere would admit
It was the source. Somewhere a distant sun
Seemed equally indifferent through haze.
A capercaillie cried out then withdrew
To be replaced by long-legged waterbirds.'

The sound of the interior

The horizon was a single endless line.
Nowhere did outcrop, rock or hill disturb
Its singularity. An evening air
Arrived to amplify the slightest sound:
At first an undivided note, a drone
Which then began, like long untwisting ropes
To separate in contrary-motion scales.

A cocoon

He heard the long horizon now vibrate
In parting strands of simultaneous airs
Like ribbons twisting round a maypole tree
Or distaff winding carded fleece to thread;
Or (even stranger image) he recalled
A plaited hammock in which once he lay,
By laughing friends spun like a silk cocoon.

Sculpture scrambling

'Inland, we drove to wait for the eclipse
And near the mountain peak parked in a square
Grassed like the elevated playing fields
Of Machu Picchu. Jane was in a mood
Of extroverted energy. She leaped
And clambered on a bronze memorial
To stand on the astronomer's outstretched hand.'

The eclipse

Experience and biography alike
Attempt to capture overwhelmingly
The feeling *All of this is happening now*
Which washes over us; this Jane felt here
Watching the molten sun in difficulties
As simultaneous strands of weft unwound
And Parcae wove the sky in which it rose.

A recommendation

'To cross the desert standing in a train
Straddling the rails at forty miles an hour
In flickering light beneath a lukewarm shower,
A golden, treeless landscape loping by,
Just visible through poorly frosted glass…
And then to read as dusk outside arrives
And settles like a dome of mica snow.'

Years of pilgrimage

'And would you say this was a time in which
You travelled merely for the sake of travel?'
'It's true that after certain losses, I
Did undertake what would become, for me,
A policy of systematic travel – yes.'
'It's been said that you seek forgetfulness…'
'No. I would say I sought *Particulars*.'

Infinitives

'To wake, the sun a fellow traveller
Above the line of slow, accompanying hills,
To see the desert red as cinnabar
The colour of one's blood, and feel the force
Between one's own containment and the vast
Ungrudging openness of passing plains
Which make no gesture to detain our flight…'

IV

Meeting

Gosse met Theophilus Zeus on board a plane,
Low flying over cinnabar terrain.
They watched a winding tracery of roads.
He had, he said, been married several times,
Now to a student, Danaë Livingstone;
He'd showered her with gold and built for her
A mansion like the one in *Citizen Kane*.

Confusion of Zeus with his namesake

'In certain places one may be aware
Of certain things. In Bourke, for instance, where
The plains prepare one for the thought of earth
As platform merely, two-dimensional,
Beneath the underbelly of the clouds,
A honey barrel on a windmill tower
Released the thought of bees and stars and Zeus.'

Bees

'Zeus, saved from Chronos and devouring time
By bees enlisted at the very mouth,
Conferred on them his immortality;
And even now, beneath a heavy sky
Which turns the plain to corrugated iron
And scatters ash against the purple hills,
They sing and dance and sow events like seeds.'

The place of mythic presences questioned

On these antipodean harvest plains,
Or in the desert once an ocean bed,
A sieve for clinker, gibber, gibberish,
Its lizard like a stick, dry, self-absorbed,
What place has Zeus and all that panoply?
Yet something in the air still sings of them
As bees burst from the silence of the hive.

Theo Zeus overbearing

As clouds dispersed outside the double glass,
Beside Gosse in the plane a seedy Zeus
Told anecdotes about his motley crew –
Of Venus careless with decolletage,
And jokes about the Gorgon's pubic hair;
Gosse was relieved to land. And there they saw
A golden fleece in every flowering gum.

Gosse Bluff

Once, in a chrome-bright airport terminal,
Drinking lime squash, he read a magazine
In which were pictures taken from above
Of Gosse Bluff looking like a splash of milk
With beaded bubbles frozen at the rim.
He flew into the sun delaying dusk;
Beside him in the window seat Zeus slept.

Sowing and harvesting

'The trouble is,' said Zeus, still half asleep,
'You want to sow and harvest at one time.
Desiring several things, all opposites,
You want to be up here enswathed with clouds
And see the river table set with trees;
And at the same time still you long to walk
Along its thorn-bush bed with swallows' nests.'

A spring wedding, Swansea, NSW

Theophilus Zeus had married in the spring
And lived that year with Danae Livingstone
At 'Highclere', Highclere Avenue, Swansea Caves;
Gosse used to visit them. 'At first I think
Danae was happy. But one day I heard
A heated argument. She used a word
I'd never heard: the *proletariat*.'

Swansea Sundays

'We used to trace the crab lines in the sand
Like time exposure light paths on the bay
When travelling craft are photographed at night.
Perhaps these canyon tracks resemble too
The lines once thought canals criss-crossed on Mars,
Or as we fly across the Bight, those roads
Mysterious, travelling nowhere, from the coast.'

From the *Swansea Gazette*

'Yes, we bought Highclere from a Doctor Zeus.
The lady left quite suddenly I think.
We lived at Leda Avenue, you see,
And used to walk that way on summer nights.
But we were not prepared for the surprise.
We'd bought the place unfurnished, yet we found
He'd left the house and in it everything…'

Everything

'The whole of everything, just as it was –
Old photographs of bridal groups; a bed;
Still on the wall a poster of the sea
With dolphins in their progress down the coast;
Even a pile of coins scattered on
The cut glass on the dressing table. And
A glass of wine, unfinished, on a chair.'

A crucial meeting

It was a few days after the eclipse
(But weeks before the comet struck the coast)
And light seemed shaken still and somewhat frail,
When in a cave at North Bondi (although
This seems less likely than a harbour bar)
Gosse met someone who knew someone who knew
The owner of two lakeside cottages.

The two houses at Conjola Lake

These houses side by side above the sea
Gosse found close to the sullen estuary
Still land-bound in the dunes. The houses' names
(In brass) were *Shangri-la* and *Tra-la-la*.
While often he would stay in *Shangri-La*
And find serenity, he sometimes came
With Celestine and friends to *Tra-la-la*.

Holidays

Here too he holidayed with Proserpine.
(Each house was then enclosed by fruiting peach,
Each tree with its long leaves like some benign
Medusa who entraps but frees the gaze).
And others travelled here to stay with him.
One winter solstice on the envious beach
Venus Marina swam without her clothes.

Between extremes

For Gosse these two blithe houses were to be
A potent influence for thirty years,
And playfully they seemed to symbolise
His movement back and forth between extremes,
Between pale sky-bliss and the sensual;
If one were being painted or repaired
The other would be waiting when he came.

Real estate opportunity

This odd caprice of naming seemed so droll
That Theo Zeus one year urged him to buy
The block of land next door ('investment-wise
A wise investment') and proceed to build
Another house of similar design –
Verandas all about, a central hall –
And plant grape vines and call it *Ooh-la-la*.

Strange conjunctions

And sometimes when he walked beside the lake
Past flame trees with cacophonies of birds
He seemed to meet, there in the she-oak's air,
Language itself. To give a trivial case:
One afternoon a storm massed overhead
And on the table, near the wooden blinds,
A *tea-cup* stood regretting it was mute.

Slow post-war recovery

Conjola Lake in 1952
Had little altered since the war's neglect;
The cormorant and pelican who sailed
With frigate-birds upstream, leaving the sea,
Then seemed to Gosse to signal something new –
If only he could read their rubric wings
Which lingered, almost falling from the sky.

A bowl of wax fruit in *Shangri-la*

Someone had left behind a centrepiece,
A brightly coloured bowl of fruit in wax,
Whose only function seemed to be to wait
In shadowy rooms for curtains to be raised
And in that smoking light suggest a past
– A wake the world's events had left behind –
Pristine, untrammelled, undisturbed, serene.

Momentous waves

The lake became a land-locked memory,
For several months cut off by sand bars, dunes;
But Gosse was present now by chance to see
The opening of the lake by heavy seas.
Momentous waves were swimming overarm
Towards the shore, then reaching it, still surged,
And broke through walls and fell upon the lake.

Jane and Gosse walk upstream

The hills were piled like melons in a bowl,
Fringed with dark slopes of ash and turpentine;
And here on certain brooding afternoons
When coastal cloud allowed a faded sun
They'd feel a dark *Gondwanaland* emerge
Intruding on the place like auk or roc
Or kangaroo sniffing the leafy air.

The *Shangri-la* experiments

On deck chairs on the wide verandah boards
Or idling in a rowing boat upstream,
He had begun those thought experiments
On differentiating thought and sleep;
On how each differs when the subject sits
Or lies, with head face down or turned…which were
The subject of an article in *Nature*.

Imminence

Gondwanaland receding at the coast
Had left Australia and Antarctica;
Gosse felt always its imminent return
Pressed at the wings abounding in the bush:
The thylacine he knew he'd meet one day
And other creatures thought extinct he sensed
Not far beyond the fringe of coastal trees.

Hinterland evening

Some poplars form a single swaying row
And each looks down the line for wayward wands.
A cricket chirrs. A flock of turning birds
Disclaims the twittering wren's predicted rain.
The fields are turf as simple as the sky:
At evening everything resolves itself
In watercolour hills and Hall Thorpe clouds.

Further upstream

A field with areas of paler grass
Like water stains in silk; a hawthorn bush;
Alongside that a tree with upstretched arms;
Alongside that, a coral tree; and then
A poplar, several Norfolk pines; a gap,
Then oleanders and a deodar;
Near them, some steps down to the lake.

Gosse makes a concession

'I always thought the painters fatuous
Who talked enthusiastically of "light"
As if a quantity in short supply
And not a swelling stream in constant flood.
Yet in the river bed the light does seem
(Despite that prejudice) as if a pump
Were forcing jets off it into the air.'

Eminence

A rainbow over humid evening fields,
A pullulation, or at least the thought
Of agitation in the valley mist,
That mist encroaching on the gilded sea…
While looking down they met a stranger who
Had thrown confetti at the wedding of
Professor Zeus and Danaë Livingstone.

V

From the *Swansea Gazette*

'The "comet" struck at last, but happily
It landed in the sea a mile offshore.
From viewing platforms improvised in haste
(Recalling those in distant memory
At Edwards Beach) observers saw the splash
Like massive dolphins leaping in a ring.
The doomsday forecasters may sleep again.'

James Benson recalls

'Not yet quite dark, the beach abstractedly
Disposed of waves; we swam expectantly.
Some said we'd feel the ocean level rise.
Some were alarmed. The thing was said to be
The size of *Shangri-la* (with balcony)
(And not of course, we learnt repeatedly,
A comet properly called). But life went on.'

Survey

A survey from a now lapsed magazine
Asked readers to contribute and recall
Where were you on the day the comet fell?
One said, 'In bed, asleep'; another said,
'Not far away. The colours were intense.'
But Gosse said, 'In the castellated shade
Made by another comet long ago.'

A summing up

'You ask me to assess what you have called
A life's achievement, estimate the lengths
To which I have succeeded in the task…
Some articles, some deferential, slight
Amendment to some marginalia –
A triumph! – Since it gladly emulates
Drops in the ocean under starry skies.'

Gosse Bluff revisited

'Can places ever be as beautiful
As we require to place such weight upon them?
When, after fifty years, I travelled there
With Theo Zeus (by now Professor Zeus)
I thought the moon gorge paled and turned away
And everywhere the clay was pastel dry…
And yet I turned to see Zeus scattering seeds.'

May

One memory supports him like a splint:
A girl is standing on a swing; the breeze
Is scarcely stirring – yet her hair perhaps
Or pinafore sways slightly, nothing more.
The background is a blue of laurel leaves,
A flame tree and a lake front, self-absorbed,
Against which like a pillar still she stands.

Near water

The long-legged heron stepping formally
Now merge in memory with long-stemmed pines
Just as a childhood memory of May
In pinafore of plaid and shining shoes
Still standing on a swing quite motionless
Has merged with others he would later know,
Until all stand on that unmoving swing.

Last visit to *Shangri-la*

Although no letters from this time survive
He may have spent one crucial season here
Between, it might be said, two memories.
He passed that winter near the river mouth
Waiting, perhaps, to be taken at the flood,
Or in a small boat, unbound to the mast,
Stood, longing for the sirens to return.

Third marriage of James Benson

After his wife's death sailing in Bass Strait
Benson had turned to ornithology
And made a study of the skeletal
Economy of pelicans, whose bones
'In flight are filled with air like honeycomb',
Then married 'someone half his age', Solange,
Who was his eldest daughter's oldest friend.

Solange

Her hair upswept and fastened with a spray
Of autumn fading blue hydrangea blooms
The colour draining from each petal's edge
With staining like the poignant pigment blur
Of salt glaze firings or of tie-dyed cloth
Reminded Gosse of stained ground where he lay
Surrounded by a circling crater wall.

Resemblance like a sword

Solange was dancing on the river lawn;
Someone was carrying glasses from the house.
She turned. Resemblance pierced him like a sword.
That she unlike should so resemble her!
That here should Jane stand now, beside the lake
At *Shangri-la*, that like and unlike should
Be so quite overwhelmingly alike!

From a letter of James Benson

'The rock face glistened from the river bank;
The wedding guests moved on the lawn. It was
A day like any other day, in that
By rearranging elements it had
Become, like every other day, unique.
We were proprietary, like clover bees,
And revelled in this day we'd gathered here…'

Jane Benson:

'He often used to talk of this: one day
(The date is unimportant and unknown)
A day occurred which he believed (or claimed
He thought) *had happened previously – entire,
Unchanged in any detail.* "Dreams!" I said,
But he said no – it was pure chance. And then
He'd smile and say, *could no one else have known?*'

Clara Wood:

'He told me something similar. One day
A car had stopped at lights. The driver and
His passenger changed places, then drove off.
He had been watching from the cypress shade
Of some grey cenotaph; that solstice day
He had the overwhelming certainty
His life had reached its midpoint on that day.'

Strange sighting

Another strange event: that same night or
Perhaps a year before (the facts are vague)
Gosse walked and passing in the lamplight's glare
He saw Danaë of twenty years before:
The indisputable face, identical
To her whom he had distantly admired
Before her meeting, luminous, with Zeus.

Obituaries of Gosse

'He was a painter without being one.
Despite some rumours of a secret work
Mysteriously to emerge after his death,
He left only some trivialities,
Some tape recordings, somewhat indistinct,
In which he drew attention to a few
Resemblances between things thought unlike...'

Further recollections

'Of course, rejecting politics he claimed,
Quite rightly in my view, that they deny
The true minutiae of constant change.
He was, we know, a masked ball devotee
And loved to talk with others also masked.
He praised cross-dressing Chevalier d'Eon...
We see here mutability at play.'

Testimonial address of Vice-Chancellor Zeus

'A painter without ever being one...
A sculptor more concerned with stone itself
Than ever making something out of it...
One day a model came; she did not pose.
Instead (and this says something of the man)
He asked her help in setting up some fruit
On tables in the bright transparent sun...'

Vice-Chancellor Zeus continues

'He taught us to enjoy diurnal change
As well as change in geological time.
He liked to see cloud shadows strafe the plain,
The wave of light traverse the stubble field.
"I'd like to see," he said to me one day
(Recalling Huysmans in a curious way)
"A chameleon moving in a stained glass light."'

James Benson waxes eloquent

'The unrecorded life retains the bloom
Of possibility. For all we know,
Gosse may have known implausible delights…
No Occam should too readily dispose
Of that mysterious three-day growth of beard
Acquired in some strange neon motel room
With swimming pool outside in bleaching sun.'

From 'Elegy for the Fifties' *(Swansea Gazette)*

'In those days (how the phrase re-echoes now)
We longed for revelation and would know
The boundaries of the individual;
To chart our innocence before the Fall
We set the self-same course. We sought a sign.
We trusted in the guidance of great men,
Ern Malley, Nietzsche, T.S. Elliot.' (sic)

Remarks of James Benson

'He nurtured and arranged experience
Like someone drying herbs. Further, I note
The same ideas persisting in his thought
For many years. So, for example, this:
A letter to his son which has survived
About the river painter Daubigny,
Ideas repeated ten years later… Thus –'

Letter to Oliver Bluff

'For painting river forests *en plein air*
The painter Daubigny planned and equipped
A floating studio-barge. And this gives rise
To the curious thought that, drifting, he must find
The river, light, the trees, all altering…
Just so, when travelling, I see myself
As an observer on that moving barge.'

Oliver Bluff recalls

'The river willow serpent, beaten gold
We followed in the truck. I opened gates
Then sprang back to the running board. We walked,
And then my father sang that plaintive song
(For which he liked to bypass melody):
"O aching beauty of the land! O slopes!
O exhalations as the plains begin!"'

Letter from Gosse to Theo Zeus

'The undulating flood plains in mild drought
Looked to the autumn willows for their life;
The ash smooth hills recalled an animal
Affectionately rolling on its back,
Legs lolling loosely; scattered trees cried out –
*Each thing it seems resembles something else
While waiting patiently to be itself.*'

An undated recollection

'It must have been in February – or in March –
Perhaps it was a little later; Easter came
And went, and autumn lined the river beds.
That morning, or perhaps the afternoon
A bay of waves like ringlets in the hair
Of Clara Wood was breaking, far offshore.
Nearby Gosse talked again of Daubigny.'

Gosse muses

'To paint the subject from a moving barge
Might seem to contradict the very claim
To Naturalism *plein air* painting makes …
And for this reason I would stroll on deck
And see the forest at its shimmering
And watch the painter, wrestling with the view,
Attempt to paint a multiplicity.'

Interlude at Lake Vanishing

Travelling down through granite-littered slopes
Gosse came upon the region loosely called
Lake Vanishing, a large plain, mountain rimmed,
Its surface velvet to the touch, inert,
A vast velour of salt with, here and there,
The arms of branches raised. And further on,
A sudden frill of fluted water moved.

Like frill-necked lizards hastening across
A heated plain, this billowing curtain edge
Of bobbing, frothing water field approached,
Its wind waves drawn down into vellum lanes.
Within the hour an effervescent lake
Had spread tarpaulins on this parchment bed.
Gosse launched the raft upon the jostling flood.

Above the bird marsh, sprays of box leaves rose
Clearing the dove grey shallows like Greek foil;
The lichen slopes which dwindled down to it
Recalled *Catullus 4* in which the word
Box-bearing, *buxifer* (used of the hill),
Suggests the adjective *buxans*, box-coloured,
Pale, to colour here this shallow lake.

Catullus listens to his whispering yacht
As its component box branch whispered once
In ancient days when it was growing still.
And Gosse lay listening as this planking nudged
The sluice of salt white shallow frothing waves,
When mingling with this sound, another came:
A motorboat approached across the lake.

It was a strange and unexpected sight.
Cutting the motor, to the deck rail strode
Theophilus Zeus, unseen for several years,
And with him at the helm Gosse was surprised
To see his (Gosse's) wife, who called, 'Darling!
I had to see you after all this time…'
(And something else the salt breeze caught and drowned.)

Zeus threw a rope and drew the two boats close
And parallel. Jane Benson joined the raft.
'I'm here,' Zeus called, 'to measure out the course
On which to try the land-speed record, or,
Should rain reanimate the lake, the same
On water. And I thought the three of us
Might picnic on these champagne-coloured banks.'

In places, salt ground rose and shallows paled;
The boats would run aground or slide and shear
And all three had to wade and push them clear.
And as they struggled Zeus said jokingly,
'It seems we need another Hercules
To bring us through mysterious springs to shore
And sunlit grasslands under conifers.'

'Ironic that we meet,' said Jane, 'in a place
Named *Vanishing*, when this has been the state
To which you have aspired. Therefore, I slept
In what once made us laugh – "night vanishing cream".
Then Zeus arrived. I dressed, and here I am…'
A genial breeze propelled the single sail.
Zeus called across the gap, 'Who brought champagne?'

Grave beauty coexisted suddenly
With light, lightness of touch (her hand on his)
And strange lightness of heart. The oars were shipped,
The rope between the two tautened then eased.
And for a while they drifted to the shore,
Each vessel independently. Gosse smiled;
They felt the subtle gravity of light.

But had there been estrangements before this?
Perhaps. Perhaps we may not ever know.
The autobiographical remains
Are thin indeed. But certainly when Zeus
Farewelled them and returned across the flood,
They hoped that they were entering a time
Of redolence, august, beneficent.

A Gruner afternoon, a Heysen dusk,
And, in between these two, the idyllic raft
Was drifting. Gosse and Jane revisited
And met the other each had known before;
Contentment now meant content blithe with form.
(A water nymph laughed briefly at the prow:
'Just checking you've sufficient space and time.')

Jane said, 'Remember what you used to say
To all the landscape painters? How you would
Infuriate them. Oh! You were severe.
You never gave them any rest. You'd say,
"And do you mean to say this patch of field
Reflecting light more brightly than the woods
Is all you offer as the *lyrical?*"'

He said, 'I knew they'd thrown away a world
Of incident, the common heritage,
Communal myth, the networks of an age,
The narrative which fused the visual,
And made us look beyond the picture plane;
And then, when Rowe Street wore the abstract crown
I wanted more than just a coloured patch.'

Healing the past perhaps, they drifted still
Until it seemed, quite unexpectedly,
Autumn. The modest air confirmed it, leaves
Were telegraphing it in poplars; Gosse
Looked up to see whole trees had suddenly
Turned gold, and heard the insistent manic cries
Of waterbirds resigned to nest elsewhere.

Across the lake the saline distance gleamed
Which is to say the glacial surfaces
Were opalescent as if seen through brine
And had that beauty which dissolves in tears…
But, more empirically, that very salt
Had concentrated in the water plain,
And orange trees were gothic with neglect.

A smell of ferment sharpened in the breeze,
The sun distilled a rustic calm. They reached
A river into which Lake Vanishing
Might once or when in flood have entered. Here
The scarecrow citrus trees tied up with rags
Stretched out of sight. The melancholy air
Released an unexpected happiness.

They took this happiness and tied it to
The supple mast. They watched it take the breeze;
It seemed to conjure in the box trees' grey
An image of Box Hill and Keats (q.v.).
Gosse could not help imposing on this screen
A European past. A breeze stirred leaves,
Von Guerard detail turned Impressionist.

The sun shook its vanilla sugar on
The pale collation of the Lake. Perhaps
Gosse slept. At least he felt that idleness
In which inconsequentials happily
Find consequence: two separate phrases, one
Only connect, the other Ripeness is all
Conjoined as Only ripen, lingering there.

Grave beauty coexisted openly
With feelings of dismay, a sense of loss
Such as a quarry sometimes seems to feel.
They looked across this lemon tinted sea
So shallow that the hull almost touched ground;
They heard the waterbirds ignoring them.
In differing ways each missed Theophilus Zeus.

The day seemed to have paused indefinitely.
And in a sun-hat, Jane, with pad and pen
Held up at arm's length pressed against the sun,
Devised an interlace for J and G.
While Gosse watched cells like froth sail down the sky,
The water level had begun to fall.
The lake was vanishing before their eyes.

And so, transparency became the rule:
The sky through which Gosse thought he saw
The gods in lazy convoys travelling;
The lake now shallow near an ancient wharf
And rusting winch and derelict launching ramp.
They talked at length of Philippa Dubois
Whom both had known once, in the flooded past.

Tabula Arata

Acknowledgements

The term is borrowed with acknowledgements
Due to our master, Ovid, who evokes
The complex furrows of the plough in clay;
And here this deep-scored tablet must depict,
(Contrasting with the *tabula rasa* grazed
By light alone, or by a sleeve erased),
                Philippa
In whose short life impulse and vision crossed
And recrossed, crowded on this furrowed ground.
We note in passing Gosse's fluttering,
Then longer friendship and still longer grief.
Criss-crossing on the snowfield of her life
Are signs of movement on that floodlit stage,
And humour too, as in the famous sketch
Of hill slope ski tracks parting round a tree.

Her parents

She liked to say in jest at river parties,
Her mother, Leda H. Dubois, née Down
Had met a certain Mr Swann.

Birth

At Delos on the theatre lawn
Miss Philippa Dubois was born
And lay on its mosaic floor.

Return to Australia

She is forgetful of all this and more
Until by ocean liner they return
To *Villa Titania*, Oberon.
There, a few leaves adhere:

First Memories

A memory of crows
Or cows
Above the weir's clay wall.

Incident in infancy

Not two years down the mirrored corridor
Attracted by the opening of a door,
Scarce walking, yet she ventured out alone,
Was plucked up by an eagle and was flown
To be set on a distant rock throne.

Sydney in the Fifties

Someone recalled a boating party, late
One summer afternoon, which possibly
She may have joined. She was fifteen:
'Wanting to find along the harbour shores
The subject of a Lloyd Rees aquarelle
We travelled slowly, unsuccessfully,
Not knowing Place to him was composite;
And all the while the wash across the bows,
And splashes on the deck dried in the sun.

We kept returning to a likely place
Only to be puzzled by a tower,
And fig trees which were there or should not be.
And Philippa, if it were she,
Trailed fingers in the wake. She seemed
More interested in water flow
Than any eminence.'

Youthful letters

In letters to her aunt, she tells
Of hopes and fears in setting out:
'My room is small, with leadlight glass
Just like your rose-lit hall.
Tomorrow I intend to find
East Sydney and perhaps enrol.'

Industrial landscape

'At Rydalmere the river teems
With simultaneous events.'
'The mangroves like camellias without flowers
Make curtains for the river's stage.'
'Gordonias, like camellias too,
But covered in camellia flowers.'
'Huge crates line every dock, a crane
Surmounts a ferry heaping them higher still.'

Resolution

'I feel that if I don't project myself
On to the passing stream of things
Then I become no one and everyone.
I'm noting down specific things
I'd like to draw or draw on for my work.'
Then follow lists, from which we quote:
'A helicopter pad with crows;
Crop dusting planes in sunset haze;
Chrysanthemums between train tracks;
A truck with broken screen. A lake;
A pony foal seen in a quarry.'
The early letters give as yet no sign
That she would hope to choreograph.
Her aunt also preserved some books
In which her niece had noted down
Ideas concerning dance. (Of these,
Extracts will follow in due course.)
But now a gulf of several years
And Gosse meets Philippa.

At the theatre

'I stood beside her at *The Winter's Tale*.
We'd rushed up to the gods and there, at last,
Breathless – like Mary Lamb's *Thank God, we are safe*
(See Lamb: *Old China*) as they reached the crest –
We looked down on the oceanic flow

Of light and declamation. Standing still
We did not speak at all till afterwards
Exultant, going down plush stairs. We talked
About the fool Leontes and the scene
In which he watches as Hermione
Steps from her pedestal and leaves the shrine –
That rapturous moment of return to life.
We talked of other metamorphoses;
I realise now I had transferred to her
The ardour of that transformation scene
And saw her stepping from a cloistered grove
As we descended through the theatre crowd…
We found for instance that we both had been
On Bondi Beach some fifteen years before
One New Year's Eve when in the afternoon
Hailstones the size of emu eggs broke through
The smoke-blue lowered ceiling, breaking heads…
The thing was quite remarkable. Of course
The same occurrence I already knew
Had struck as Benson backed a lakeside truck;
The windscreen cracked, he'd panicked at the shock
Of ice and glass deposited on him
As if a silver tray of drinks upturned.
Philippa recalled the bruising sky
And people running in and out of waves.
What's more, we found we both knew Theo Zeus.'

Ocean of Memory

Luxuriating in the magic realm
Of multiple coincidence we swam
From shore to luminous shore, busy with waves,
And climbed on to a tilting, moored pontoon
In whose bright sun, feeling its waves beneath,
We smiled to see our intersecting lives.
We parted near the entrance to St James.

Nepean landscape

'I imagine dancers on the river bank,
The Lewers garden like a complex stage
With backdrop from the Rowe Street gallery.'

The river

'The long Nepean takes its time to leave
The Lewers house and reach the Emu weir
And then beyond the Yarramundi bridge
Becomes the Hawkesbury. And in all of this
One senses dancers on its tidal stage.'

Galleria recollections

The Browser in the Dictionary was then
A shadowy figure in our circle. For,
As he himself said frequently, he was
'A sometime infrequenter of your haunts'.

He always was quite prolix, most polite,
Professing sentiments appropriate
But took some time to reach the point
If ever point were reached. For instance, once
Waylaying us near Argyle Cut (the steps)
He launched into some thoughtful monologue
Concerning time (itself notoriously
A topic both obscure and difficult):

An Ancient Mariner

'I do apologise for mentioning
That most elusive, vacuous of words
But I could not help noting in the swell
Of things transpiring since the sun leapt up
Real time had once again won out and led
And left behind, by some small interval,
Each counterpoising simulacrum. Well!
In fact to speak of time I thought I should
Avoid the word completely and perhaps
Attempt the indirectness of Charades:
My first is in teetering, toppling, tears;
My second is myself, my inner eye;
My third and fourth together constitute
My self as target of all happening.
But I digress. You've asked me to recall;
In answer to your cries importunate,
I did in fact speak to the lady named.
I only met her twice or, should I say,
I met her only twice. Once was above

The *Galleria* in an upper room.
An upper room! Now there's a potent phrase
To conjure with – a wind blows through that room:
It was, I think, her own *tableau vivant*
(Though why *vivant* when everyone is still?)
The kind of thing she liked, although she liked
Configurations of kinesis more,
Not stillness posed as history. But still,
Its subject was pale Dido and Aeneas
And ended with the famous harbour scene,
Aeneas leaving Carthage and his queen
At the remonstrance of the gods. He sails,
Looks back and sees a fire, unaware
That this is Dido's pyre. This was, I think,
Philippa's triumph. Unmoving through that death
(Behind red cellophane) she moved us all.
The second, since you press me further still,
Was in a storm at Bondi, in a cave.
We met by chance, both sheltering from the hail
(As Dido and Aeneas had to do).
No doubt the potent mention of a cave
Will have you soon invoking Forster's cave
(We'll leave out Plato if you will…)
Well, I'm not saying any more. The cave
Was dark yet luminous. We spoke, I think,
After the storm had passed, *about the dance.*'
The Browser in the Dictionary concludes
With one last lurch towards irrelevance:

Pursuing the retreating wedding guest

'But one thing more I'd like to say
Although not strictly relevant
(Concerning as it does a hill
At dusk, superbly resonant).
I know that nowadays we choose
To call in doubt the beautiful
Fearing our subjectivity,
Wanting the concrete edifice.
Yet when I saw at last the clouds
Turn flesh of cantaloup and fade
Against a Cycladean blue
I could not see how to describe
The presence of this complex mass,
The hills with fimbriate sky-washed trees.
Prolonging dusk by climbing still
Through sequences of locks, we saw
Dusk's last disclosures till, too soon,
The road beside our boat seemed gone.
If you want relevance, then say
That *Philippa* should have been here.'

A paucity of facts

Rumours concerning Philippa Dubois
Suggest that once she may have been involved
In what Fordyce in trying to avoid
All mention of some base Catullan themes
Denotes 'immoderate proclivities'.
These cannot be denied, but equally
Are not with any certainty confirmed.

The exercise books

Her aunt preserved a notebook in her hand.
It has this title scribbled on one page,
Infinitives.
It might be said that this prefigures well
Their status: *unfulfilled*.
These entries tell us something of her hopes:

'*To* fast in search of visions. How control?
To make plain flour from acorns? Check.
To specify kinetic grace. Notate?
To pace the many-sided field, then place
It like a handkerchief upon the head
And walking carry it from fence to fence.
To walk like cats across a narrow wall.
To choreograph the courtship dance of men.'

Then follow many brief scenarios:

'The *ballet of* the trees hunched round the stream.
The *ballet of* the trees in autumn change.
The *ballet of* the paddock's single tree.
The *ballet of* the fruit grouped in a bowl.
The *ballet of* the seated banquet guests.
The *ballet of* the swimmer in a pool.
The *ballet of* the sculpture being carved.
The *ballet of* the bifurcating branch
And river parting round the wooded isle.
The *ballet of* the shoreline fisherman.
The *ballet of* the mirror in the room.
The *ballet of* the sunlight near its shade.

The *ballet of* the thoughts lost in the sun.
The *ballet of* the mangrove without flowers.

The *ballet of* Lady Ottoline Morrell –
I love being really rather gorgeous.

The *ballet of* Irregularity:
Remember Gosse describing childhood games
And country football dodging round a tree.

The *ballet of* the tram that got away
At Athol wharf not far from antelopes.'

Testimony of Jane Benson

'Of course she would have done it all,
I have no doubts. I knew her well.
She had such energy.
Her fondest project, I believe,
And now a matter for regret,
At its loss, was this:
*The ballet of the substratum
In which events, like plants, inhere.*'

A difference of opinion

'I disagree. She spoke to me at length.
I think her major dance work may have been
Leda Under the Embracing Wing.'

A further contender

'Another ballet, based on Sterne
(A writer who had made her laugh),
Was called *A Sentimental Tale*:
Asides and indeterminacies,
Interpolations, change of mind,
Reluctance to be definite
Or to pursue a single line
Are mirrored by the dancers, thus
Kept to a multiplicity
By systematic indecision.'

Her humour noted by various witnesses

'I'd see her coming out of sombre woods
With one or other of her student friends,
Preoccupied with laughter, looking up
As one imagines *Penelope* unravelling
The day's events, engrossed, preoccupied.'

A waiter's recollection

'Once in the Restaurant Apollo, where
All food and drink was served in glass, and where
She liked to go, I heard her laugh
So suddenly, so operatically
A champagne glass was shattered by the sound,
At which the entire company laughed.'

A Krishnamurti student comments

'She'd sink into a silence, but we knew
This was no melancholy reverie,
But rather, like a diver in a bell
Descending to survey the silent world
She'd smile at self-referring sequences
And contradictory statements from this world
Which seemed to swim against the dome of glass.'

Letter to Jane Benson

'I wanted to invent
The dance which would make people smile and laugh
Without their ever knowing why…
A product of the space
Between the dancers… But you understand.'

She is remembered at the Simone de Beauvoir Society

'She found (although she did not speak of it)
A cure for existential angst,
Others as Other, Self opposing them,
By means of laughter in the dance she called
How humorous that we should both be here.'

A fondness for sight gags

'I think that if she faced a whitewashed wall
She'd see it as a backcloth. *Harlequin*
Would come on running, dive into a trunk
Whose lid would shut, just when old *Pantaloon*
Had turned to some disturbance in the yard
And *Columbine* was signalling to the wings.
Concerted action was to her, *per se*,
Amusing, since the simultaneous
Seemed like a kind of virtuosity.'

Her death

'How did we lose her? Will we ever know?
At some time in the period
In which the Moon Landing was watched
By millions on their moon-grey screens
Philippa Dubois, apparently,
Vanished from the face of the earth.'

A questionable claim

'She died in my garden on the gravel path
Precisely at the place where she had staged
Her dance in which Prometheus steals fire
Then stays to guarantee the host flame lives.'

Star sonnet

'A little while ago I was informed, by friends
Of the deceased (who wish to be anonymous),
Of something which to me speaks volubly of her,
And so it seems appropriate that I should share
This with you all. Imagine if you will her room:
The simple bed, the photograph of Balanchine.
Its ceiling wore a galaxy of stars, cut out
From phosphorescent paper. These she had attached,
And every night extinguishing her lamp she'd lie
And watch this glowing, scintillating Milky Way.
And so, my friends, on this sad day I'd like to think
That we could see this ceiling, flickering, immense,
As shining on us all, and in some way a sign
And, yes, a symbol, of her own aspiring life.'

Eulogy

'Few people will have heard of Miss Dubois.
This must not be allowed to tell against
The promise of her youth, that blazing star
Consumed in its own fire. Rather let
Us see her stillness now as momentary:
The painter *Artemisia Gentileschi*
Depicts herself caught in the allegory
Of Painting; so we may see *Philippa*
Arrested in that instant in the dance
When stillness interposes radiance
Between two moments. Such epiphanies
She sought to specify, proclaim, set down,
Invent and order in a timeless frieze.

To choose to fashion movement is to use
A medium impermanent, invisible;
To add her own invisibility
Expresses this quintessence. Let us then
Assume she has achieved an entrechat
So startling, so illustrious, so sublime,
That she has left all gravity behind
And leapt into the festive, humorous clouds.'

Recollections of Hugh Edwards

Hugh Edwards, born in Gulgong, NSW,
Was, from an early age, ingenious;
His father had been influential in
The rally which became the Coo-ee March,
And to his son bequeathed *enthusiasm*.
(That glittering arc, advancing joyfully
Would prove a sputtering fuse soon to explode
With blinding radiance in a poppy field.)

He'd seen the Loire before he reached the Somme
And written, to the boy, of structures, sights
As glorious as the luminiferous dusks
Like pollen dust on their own Western Slopes.
At Flanders he had talked with Rupert Brooke;
His son preserved a folded envelope
Which bore, beside that luminary signature,
An enigmatic drawing of the coast.

The boy read avidly and showed some signs
Of eccentricity, devising schemes
For separation of the cream from milk
Using the sun, for making wine from flowers;
He manufactured fireworks (and burned
By accident a slab built shed), theorised
On colour sense in farmyard animals.
He often thought about the Coo-ee March.

Between his time at university
(Which he prolonged by always carefully
Avoiding sequences) and what would be
Vague, intermittent periods of 'work',
He spent much time and effort to promote
A re-enactment of the Coo-ee March.
The thing obsessed him. It would be in part
A re-enactment, part a surge of faith.

He fished at Circular Quay: he cast a line
Then cast about for what might galvanise
A people in the apathy of peace.
He needed some as yet unformed idea
To bind once more the swelling, singing throng
Of people gathering from the countryside
And people greeting them in glowing towns,
Romance born in that fierce communal gaze.

At length this idea faded. In its place
Another drew its shape from Arthur Stace:
An inventory of his Eternity,
A public poetry, anonymous
As unexpected. This must be his task.
And after that decision for three days
He felt elation, certainty, the calm
Of Fermat's secret, unrecoverable proof.

'One morning it began when I awoke
Somewhere near Cadman's Cottage where I lay;
The thought came to me, floating, "Caedmon's hymn!"
I would hereafter emulate his dream
His version of the book of Genesis,
To say nothing (or almost nothing here)
Of Cadmus and Harmonia bringing Thebes
The alphabet! I thought I'd do the same.

Near Cadman's Cottage at the water's edge
An upturned tanker lay for several weeks,
A rusting surface raised for all to read!
While Arthur Stace discreetly worked his way
From Darlinghurst to Martin Place I'd stay
Near Circular Quay and wield my copperplate
And chalk such words across this carapace
To discombobulate the populace.'

At first he thought in terms of others' words,
Of Djuna Barnes for instance, new to our shores,
Perfumed like guava, wrapped in powdered silk,
A mystery delicious as a fruit –
And so, one morning, ferries passed these words:
The vision of an eland coming down
An aisle of trees, chapleted et cetera,
A hoof raised in the economy of fear.

'Now that *economy* was poetry!
Just as was *chapleted with orange blossom
And bridal veil.* And so, for several days,
I savoured this effusion thus proclaimed
Against the glittering harbour and its shore.
To see such radiance from the Balmain ferry!
Yes, I would travel too, imparadised
In delectation's haze to read it there.'

After a time he'd chalk another text
Delighting always in the aureate,
Increasingly inclining to his own
Inventions – aphoristic, lyrical:
'The words should gleam like middens which the tide
And morning sun uncover on the shore.'
Before first light he'd write the latest lines,
Then linger still beside the glowing hulk.

Eventually the wreck was towed away.
He walked there with regret. The sky seemed blank,
The sea a *tabula rasa* once again,
A sense of loss returning with each tide.
But then he found a warehouse wall, ideal
In that it bordered on a playing field
Beside a railway line. Here he began
His over-zealous *Fragments from the Zone.*

Subversive poetry appealed to him
Whose father had espoused the public good
And marched through Mudgee with fallacious Hope
And revelled on the slopes of Mystery Hill
And in the coal sweet air of Lithgow laughed,
And slept with dark-eyed Possibility,
Only to wake and find her gone. Perhaps
The son was writing letters from the Front.

He liked the chalk's persistence after rain;
He liked the empty wall still wet with dew;
He liked the pavement pitted with the Past.
The *Fragments* had increasingly become
Erratic, free, oblique – clearly derived
From ex-Professor Brennan's manuscript
In imitation of *Un Coup de Dès*
Which he had seen in rooms at Paddington.

The life conceived in hope may bury hope
Which yet may spring in labyrinthine forms.
If Hamlet and Lear embody gaiety
Then H.R. Edwards soared to heights of joy.
He did not marry, lived the life unknown
And wrote of vistas on ephemeral shores:
His most serene sensation may have been
Tactilities of chalk on dew-wet walls.

Appendix: Further Fragments

Possible contacts

Advertisements resulted in a yield
Of further fragments. One is typical.
'I think the Philippa you're searching for
I met in fact by chance one frosty night.
A bomb scare at the Independent had
Ejected us, from *Huis Clos* inside
To glittering headlight flares mingling outside
In Miller Street. We laughed. Someone had wine.'

A poor opinion of Sartre

'And, well – I also wondered at the time –
Whoever telephoned and got us out
Perhaps shared my opinion of that play
And wanted something looser, more informal,
As certainly we found here as we milled
About in Miller Street, the traffic stopped,
A taxi driver strolling from his cab
As Philippa danced on its glistening hood.'

A mêlée

'Zigzagging in the snow or standing still,
In those days everyone, it seemed to me,
Was travelling with Gurdjieff – Orage
For instance in his aphorism, *Be
A pianist and not a piano.* Yet
In this mêlée still blocking Miller Street
We all were played upon, were sounding-boards
For concertante impromptus from the sky.'

Presence of mythic elements

'Mourning the death of Rowe Street I had found
A bar, and Edward Edwards, scientist,
A second cousin twice removed from Hugh.
He drank. We talked. He said, "The air is thin.
Through it we see the curvature of space
Producing hoardings which proclaim our myths."
"As Hugh McCrae," I said, "at River Road
Saw satyrs on the forehead of the air."'

Edward Edwards proves as expansive as his cousin

'Each moment like a cell of D.N.A.
Will shape our lives in some specific way.
One cell is calibrated to allow
The taste of raspberries. Another tells
The ear to note a saddening minor third;
Another gives the hills their shade of blue.
Our moments too, perhaps twice helical,
Divide and climb round us like eglantine.'

New-laid eggs

'I went to take a dozen new-laid eggs
To an address in Bondi Junction. As
I knocked I heard the sound of scuffling, cries
And laughter. No one came. I rang the bell
And stepping back looked up. The sparrows' eaves
Were empty. Passing in the street, a car.
The door yielded. Two men were wrestling. One
Named Jacob smiled and drew a map for me.'

Foreknowledge in Philippa Dubois

'That's strange,' said Jack (James) Benson. 'In her book,
You say there's evidence she'd seen the truck
Abandoned by the lake. When I got back
The truck had come to rest against a rock
Which wasn't there before. Picture my shock!
Someone perhaps had moved it – or the lake
Had suddenly withdrawn. Still, that would make
Her note pre-date that famous hail attack.'

Another instance

'One would have thought so. Yes, and what is more,
She wrote, "Hydrangea flowers in autumn lose
Their pigment back into the stem; a stain
Like rust in streams remains, just as
Blue cornflowers in a vase will, over days,
Lose all their colour back into the vase."
Now this is strange. She must have written that
Before I saw the cornflowers at Jane's house.'

From the Acme Boat Hire Co.

'Dear Mr Bluff, Our hiring records show
That at the time of writing you have not
Returned the coracle named *Saucy Sal*...'
Could this be Gosse? We know he used to row
In Middle Harbour in those middle years –
('We tied up at the pier with dragonflies;
The shallows lapped at white-mown buffalo grass.
A flag flew from the castellated tower.')

In search of the real Philippa Dubois

'Describe her? Well, if we are talking here
About the same Miss Philippa Dubois,
I've heard it said she was in many ways
Like Ingrid Bergman in her Renoir film,
In which the smile belies a rich distress.
But Philippa like Ingrid Bergman? Well, she had
That certainty of gaze, but I would say –
More like Joan Crawford wading out to sea.'

Useless information

'She had indeed a gravity such as
One might see in a Courbet cliff face; or
Perhaps it was a prescience of hers
That much which she aspired to choreograph
Would have to move itself without her help.
Her eyes? A violet blue, I think. Her hair,
Although she wore it short, was – auburn, yes,
I'm sure of this. How well it framed her face!'

A Discourse on Method by Hugh Edwards

'I'd always thought of happenings or "events"
As subjects for investigation. First
I'd question how they float and in what sea
And next try to be there as they recede.
For instance, as I walk across a lawn
Outside the Polytechnic, two silk dogs
Break from their owner playfully and run
Towards me. She calls, and stands up as I turn.'

The Method refined

'Consider the event which seems to have
No visible concomitant. I mean
The thing which seems to happen *carefully*
Without proliferation on all sides.
For instance, take the gentle, frothing wave
Which once I saw advancing on its own
Along the river bed still dry with drought
When far away there had been heavy rain.'

Red-brick flats

'My father took me to the red brick flats
Near Edwards Beach; the artists' camps were here,
And more – the Amphitheatre too, where stood
The faithful under cloudy skies to see
Young Krishnamurti walking on the sea.
I climbed the steps and walked about the roof:
Geranium overran the garden urns.
I thought I saw a sail beyond the Heads.'

Idle speculation

'The sun came out quite searingly, the heat
Burned our bare heads although the month was May;
A conifer surprisingly turned gold.
I'd come back to the Amphitheatre site.
Someone had fallen from this roof, someone
Who thought of dancing on its parapet.
Had this been Philippa? I thought. But no –
Her Krishnamurti phase passed long ago.'

A Phenakistoscope or Gosse suffers love at first sight

'Did its inventor ever realise
How closely this mechanical device
May come to representing how we live?
The slit through which we see its passing world
Is like *the present*... But I see you know.
James Benson had one once. He showed me how
The handle made the world rotate. I stared;
I thought I saw his sister in a street.'

Car phone

'Vanilla Reith-Jones rang me from her car,
Crossing the city. Every underpass
Caused interference. Still, I heard her say,
"...I thought you'd like to know... Remember Jane?
I have just heard the most amazing thing!
(You wouldn't want to know! The road is blocked
By someone waving a strelitzia)
... Jane's travelling round the world with Theo Zeus."'

She continues

'Her brother James died recently... You'd heard?
By falling from a waterfall! Yes, sad.
He always was a darling, even if
A bit sententious, if that is the word.
One thing obsessed him – as I now recall:
He always said, *Always avoid the use
Of Symbolism at all cost.* He said
He wanted everything to be itself.'

Proliferation

A mass of fragments, all that now remain,
Includes the fact that Clara Wood liked ducks
And fed them in Centennial Park. As well,
Hugh Edwards, it was said, kept them as pets,
And one particular favourite used to sit,
Held on his lap, and liked the radio.
James Benson liked the symphonies of Brahms
And wrote a stern rebuke to G.B. Shaw.

Fragments without constraint

'At length I left, and learned to live without
The mothering landscape. Sadness wrapped me then
In its intolerable swaddling… Then I knew
That I could neither leave nor properly stay.'
'… The truck is gone. The lake recedes. Near rocks
The ibis in their dust coats pace about.'
'… She even wanted me to give myself
That she might choreograph our every move.'

Structure, not *facts*: an envoi

… And so on, endlessly. Such facts if found,
Unbounded may yield less rather than more
Of lives which grow like fruiting trees, whose laws
Are all-pervasive if invisible.
The double helix made of ping-pong balls,
Each sphere a fact, is locked away. Instead
We write across the blackboard Hölderlin's
To live? To live is to protect a form.

www.ingramcontent.com/pod-product-compliance
Lightning Source LLC
Chambersburg PA
CBHW070049120526
44589CB00034B/1655